Clare Beaton's

MAKE AND COLOUR

PAPER PLANES

b small publishing

How to use this book

• On the black and white centre pages are ready-drawn planes for you to colour and fold. Remove these pages first: place the book on a flat surface and ask an adult to help you open the staples. Carefully pull out the pages, then close the staples again. Cut each page in two along the line marked.

• Colour each plane with felt-tip pens, crayons or coloured pencils before folding it. See page 8 for more ideas.

• Use the stencils inside the back cover to decorate the wings and fuselage.

• On the inside of the back cover there is a chart to keep a record of plane races with your friends.

Keep the rest of the book. It has instructions on how to fold the planes, plus lots of tips on how to fly them. There are also ideas for plane decorations.

Some things you will need:

- plain or coloured A4 paper
- crayons, coloured pencils, felt-tip pens
- paper clips
- sticky tape
- pencil and tracing paper
- scissors
- thread
- sticky shapes

Templates

You can make plane mobiles using the templates inside the front cover. See page 8 for instructions. Here is a way to trace from the plane templates very simply and successfully.

What you will need:

- tracing paper
- soft pencil
- sticky tape
- stiff paper or card

1 Tape a piece of tracing paper over the templates, then trace over a shape with a pencil.

2 Turn over the tracing paper and scribble over the lines with a soft pencil.

3 Turn over again and tape on to a piece of card. Retrace over the lines firmly. Remove the tracing paper.

Stencils

Cut along the perforated line to remove the sheet of stencils from the back cover. See pages 7 and 8 for ideas on how to use them to decorate your planes.

What you will need:

- paper
- pencil
- scissors

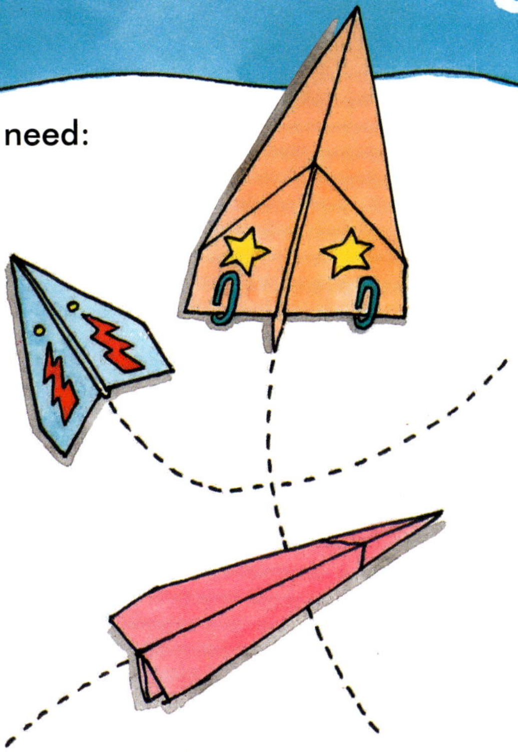

Place the stencil shape on the plane or sheet of paper. Draw inside the shape with a pencil.

Colour in the shape, or cut it out with scissors.

Tips on folding and flying planes

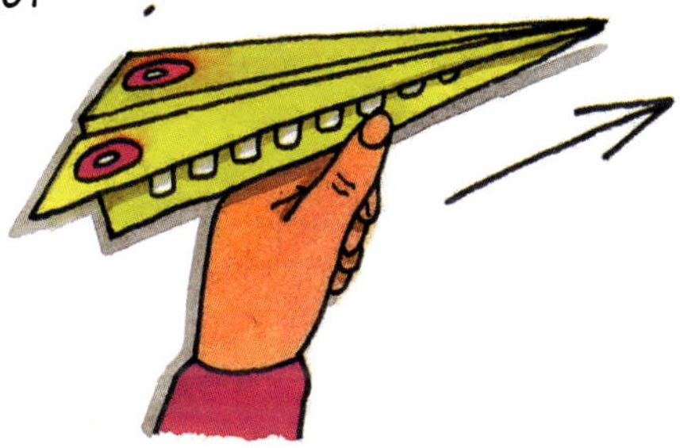

Work on a clean, hard, flat surface. The more care you take, the better your plane will fly, so it is important to fold accurately and neatly and to follow the instructions. Make sure the edges and corners of the paper meet where they should before you press down and crease the paper.

You can alter our basic designs to create your own planes. Make them simpler or more complicated to see how they fly. Experiment with papers and colour schemes, too.

Photocopier paper is very good, but try others. If you make your own planes, you will have to colour them after you've made them, so take care not to crumple them at the decorating stage.

Launch your plane by holding it between your thumb and forefinger, about 12 cm away from your nose. Throw the plane gently, moving your whole arm. You can experiment launching the plane at different angles. For example, try a slight tilt upwards.

You can adjust the way your plane flies by tearing flaps in the back of the wings, or you can weight the nose or wings with paper clips.

Run your fingernail along the folds to make them crisp and neat.

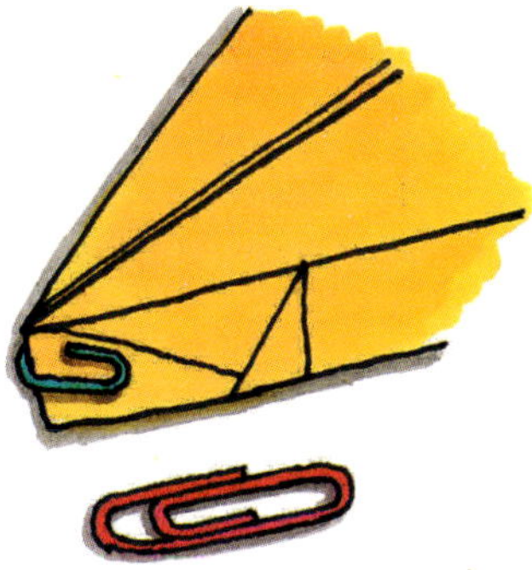

Folding planes

Decorate the white areas of the pull-out planes before you start folding – the grey areas will not show once the planes are folded. Then fold a crease along the dotted centre line on each plane and place the page 'front' face-up. Follow the instructions below. The dotted fold lines will guide you.
For more tips, see page 3.

Classic Dart

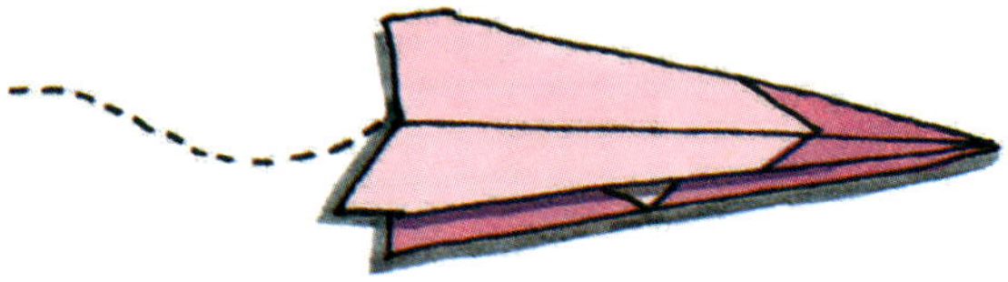

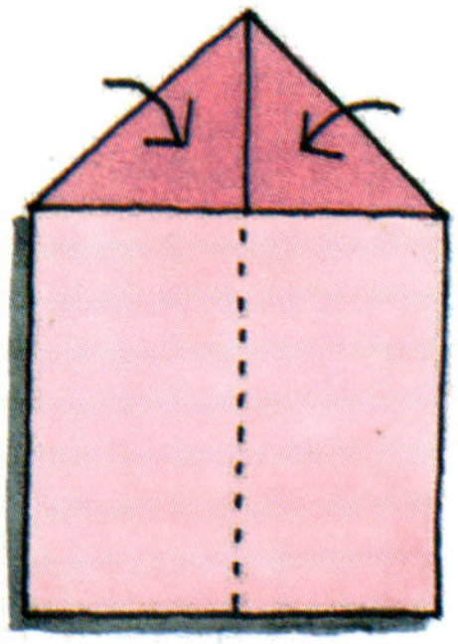

1 Fold top corners inwards to centre.

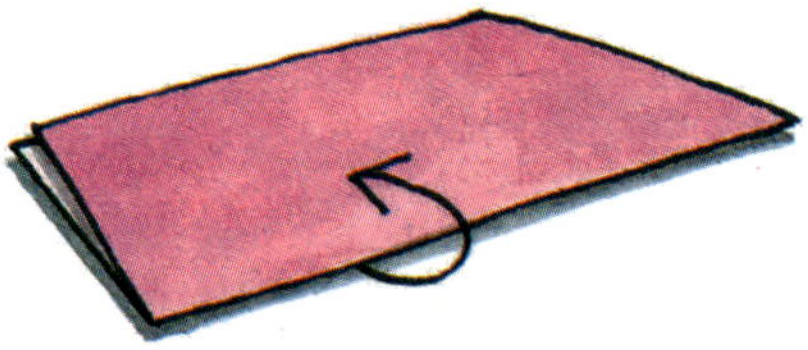

2 Fold in half inwards, along centre line.

3 Fold down wing to meet bottom fold.

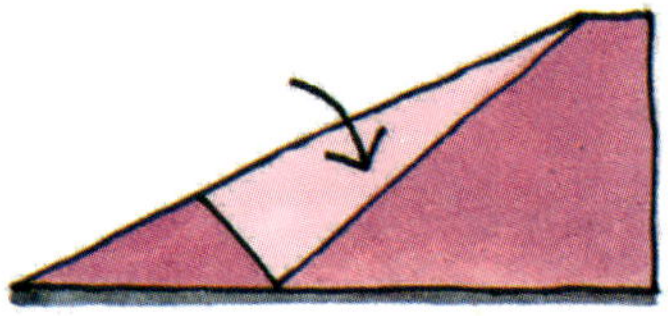

4 Turn over. Fold down second wing to match.

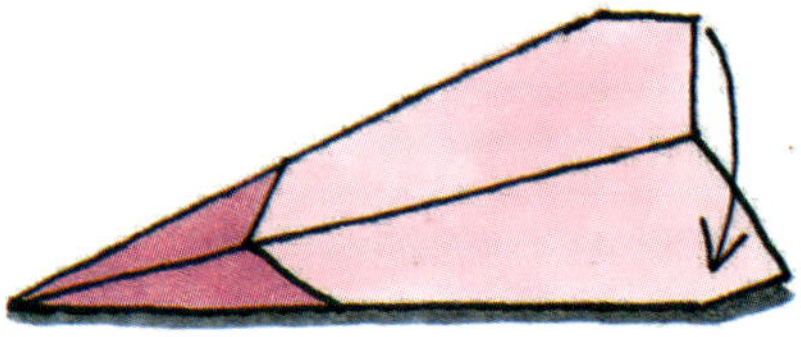

5 Fold down wing again, to meet bottom edge.

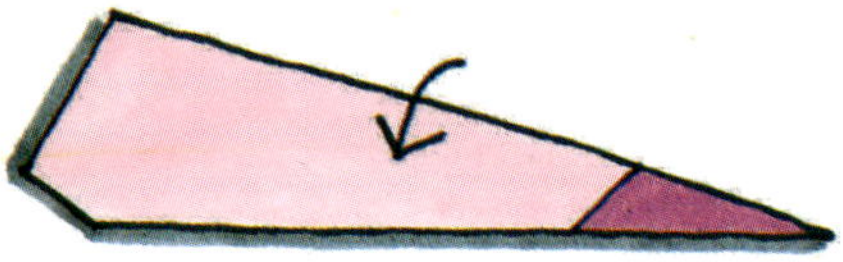

6 Turn plane over. Fold down other wing.

Silver Arrow

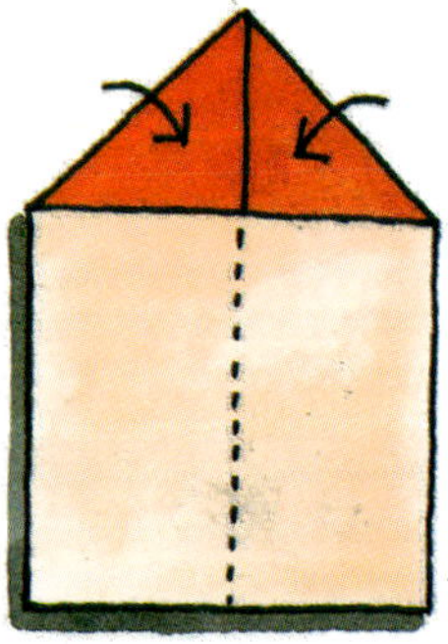

1 Fold top corners inwards to centre.

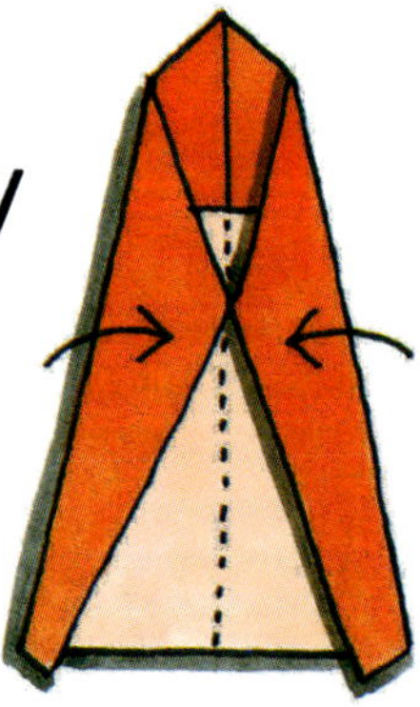

2 Fold in sides along dotted lines. Make sure points meet in centre.

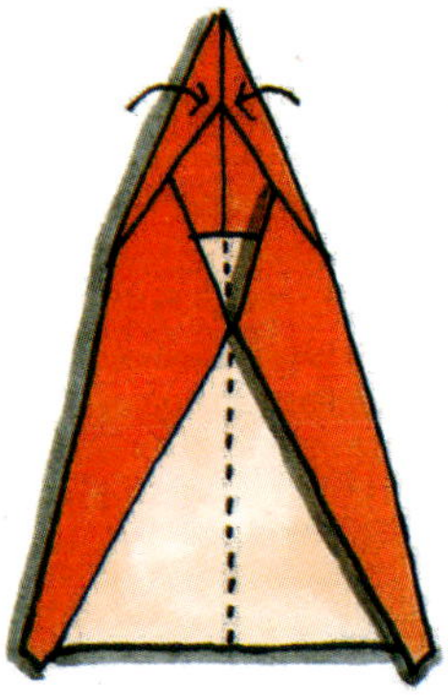

3 Fold in sides from top point. Make sure they meet in centre.

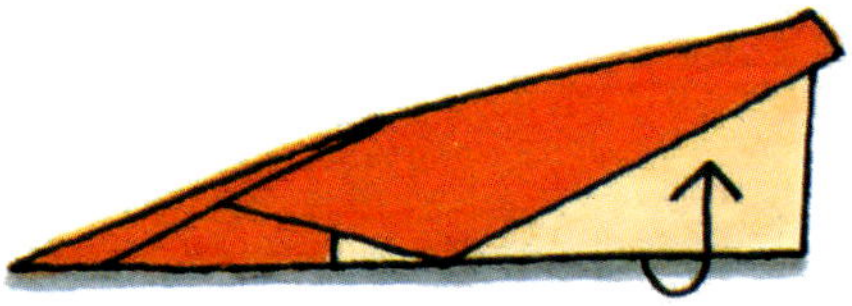

4 Fold in half outwards along length.

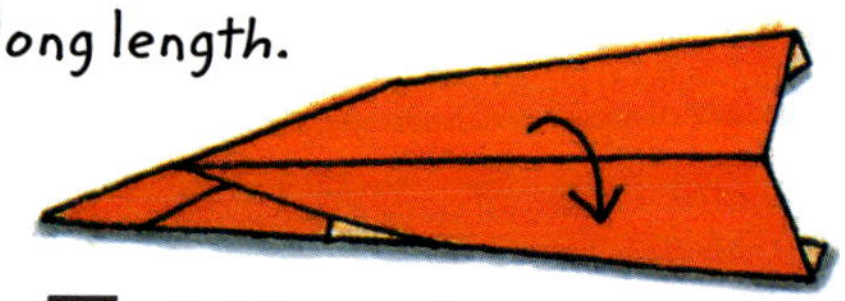

5 Fold wing down to line up with bottom edge.

6 Turn over. Fold down second wing.

Glider

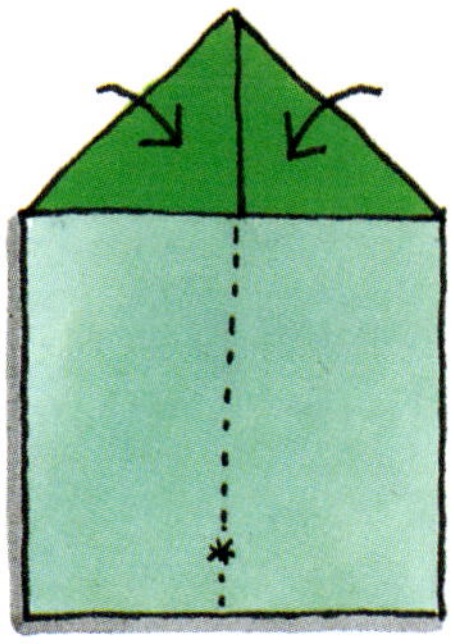

1 Fold top corners inwards to centre.

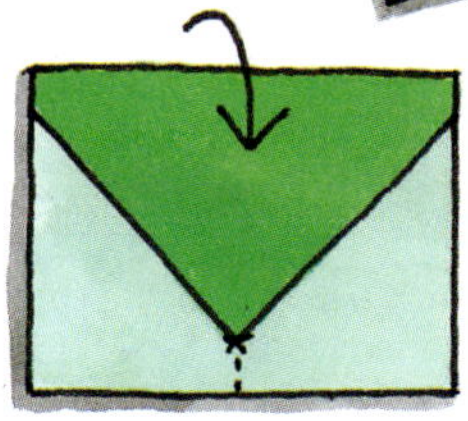

2 Fold down top half of paper so point meets star.

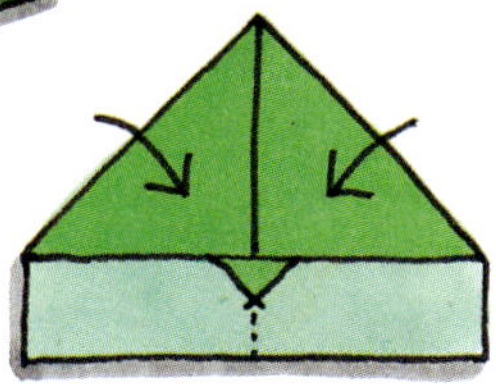

3 Fold top corners inwards to meet at centre.

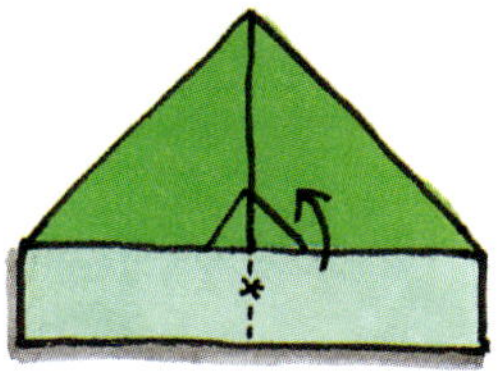

4 Turn small triangle up over corners.

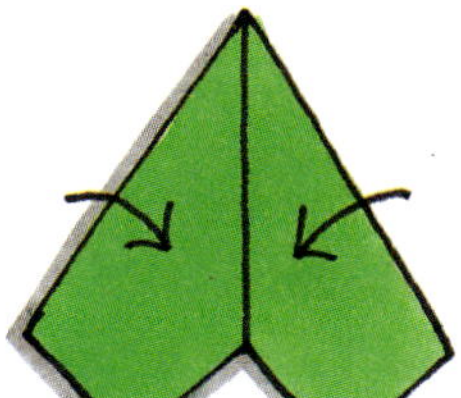

5 Fold sides inwards to meet at centre.

6 Fold in half outwards. Open wings up to sides.

Concorde

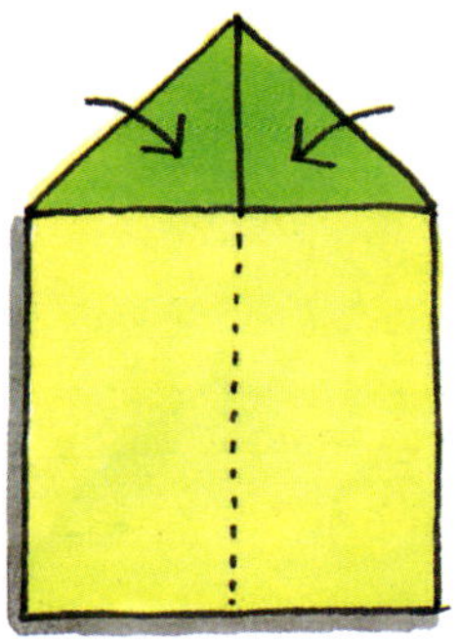

1 Fold top corners inwards to centre.

2 Fold sides in again, to meet in centre.

3 Fold in half inwards along centre of length.

4 Fold down wing, parallel to bottom edge.

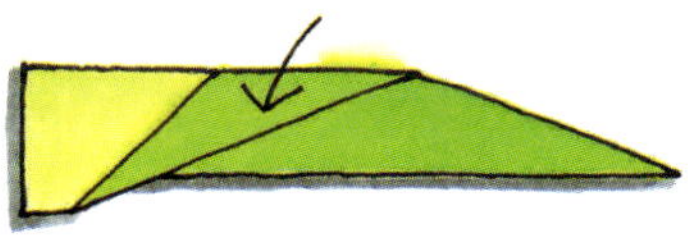

5 Turn over. Fold down the other wing to match.

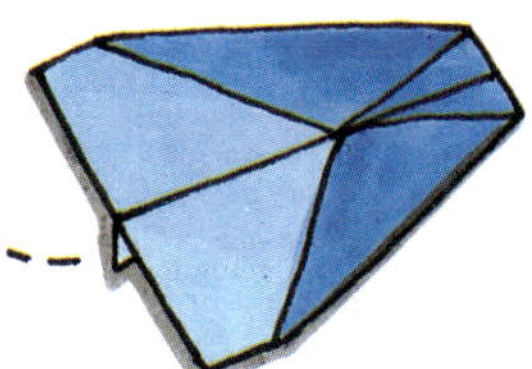

Stubby

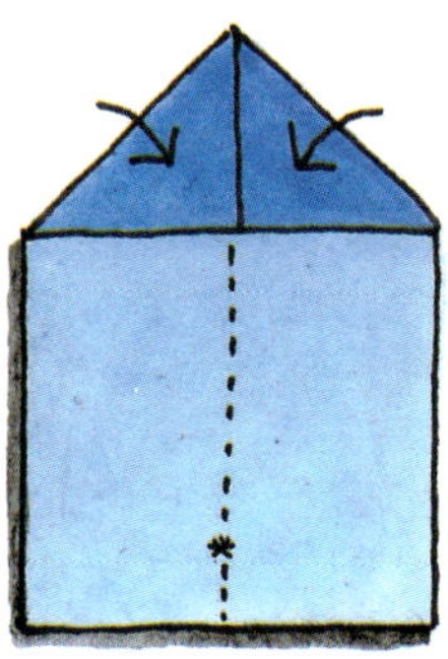

1 Fold top corners inwards to centre.

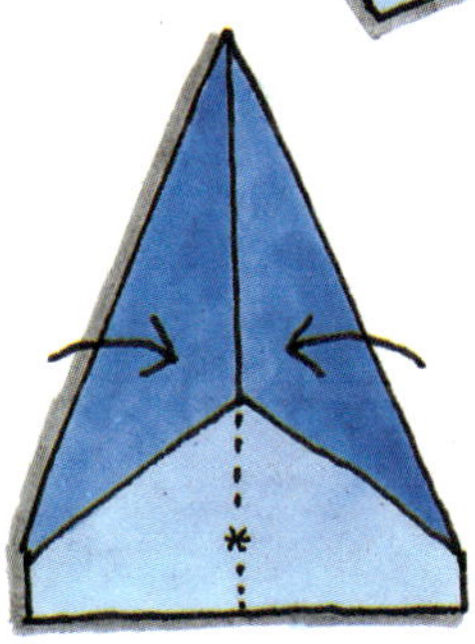

2 Fold in sides to meet at centre.

3 Fold top point down to meet star.

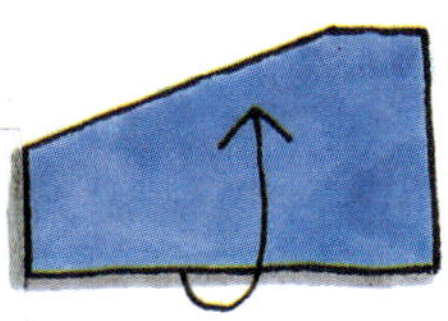

4 Fold in half inwards along length.

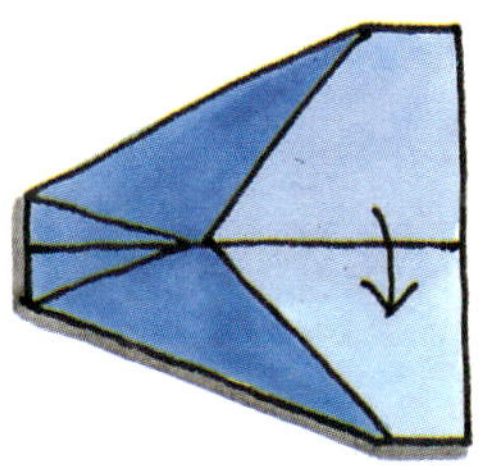

5 Fold down wing along dotted line.

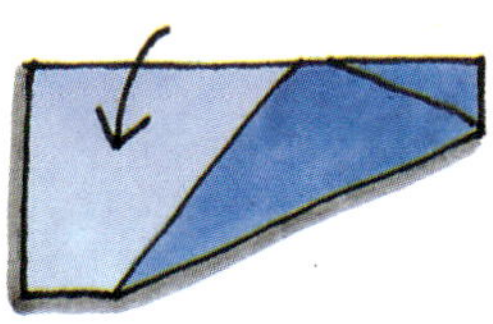

6 Turn over. Fold down second wing.

Cloud Skimmer

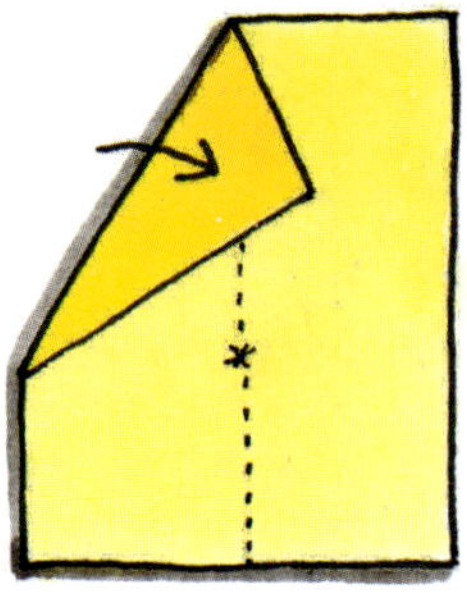

1 Fold top left corner over along dotted line.

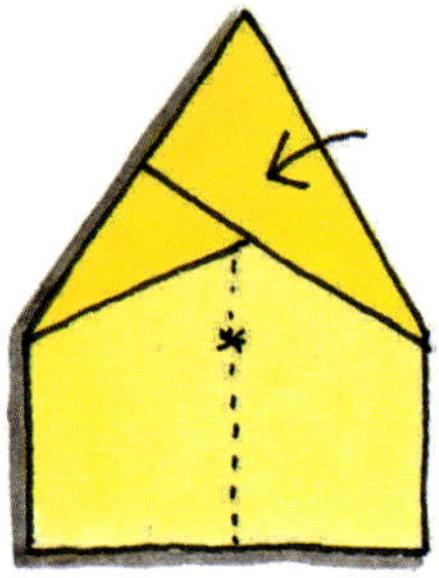

2 Fold over other corner.

3 Fold down top point to meet star.

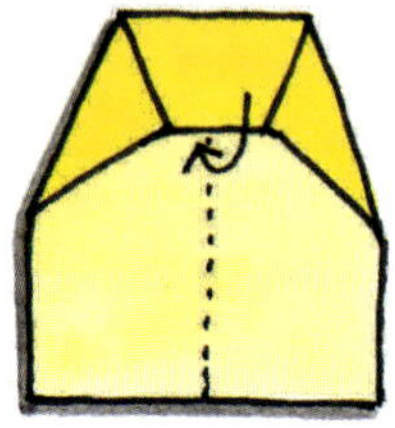

4 Fold point under the folds.

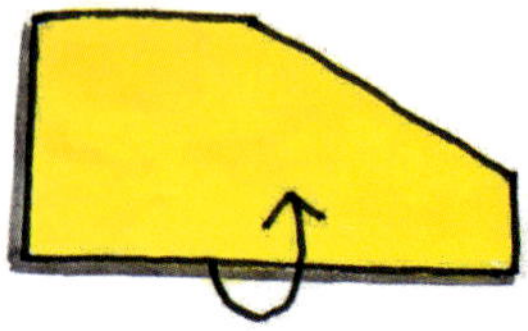

5 Fold in half along length.

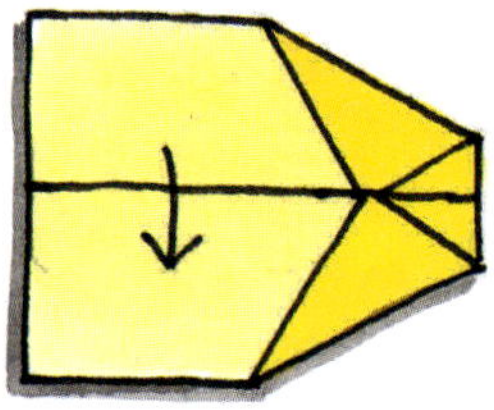

6 Fold down wing along dotted line.

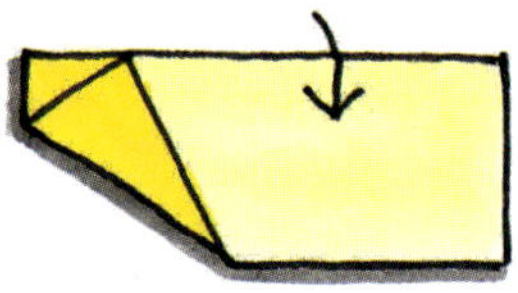

7 Turn over. Fold down second wing to match.

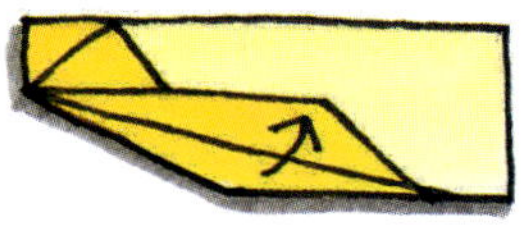

8 Fold up flap along dotted line.

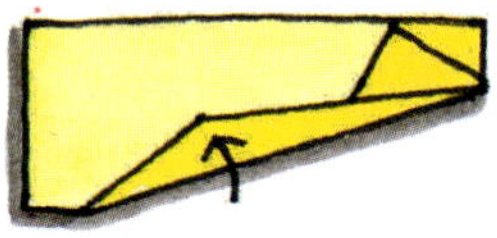

9 Turn over. Fold up second side to match first one.

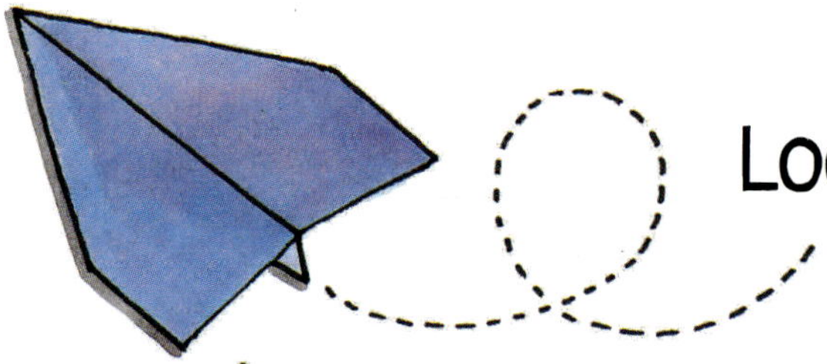

Loop the Looper

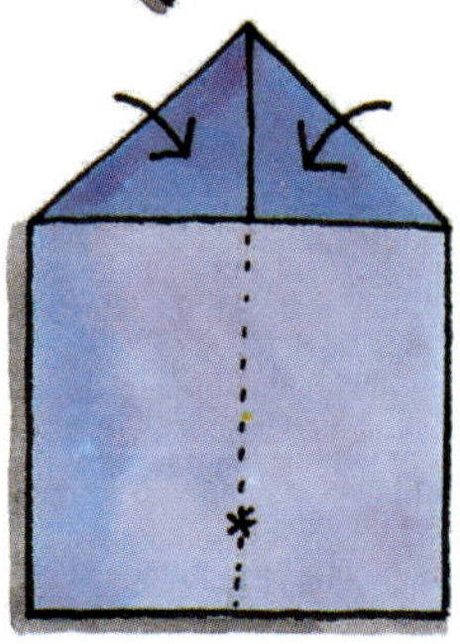

1 Fold top corners inwards to centre.

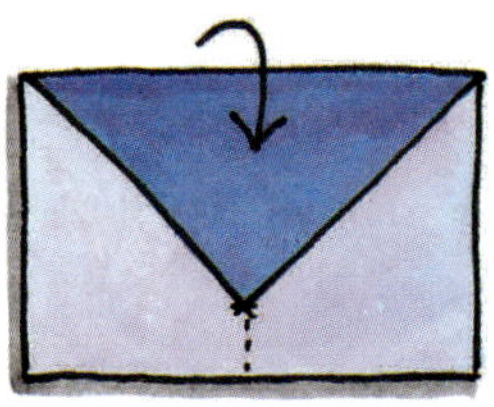

2 Fold top point down to meet star.

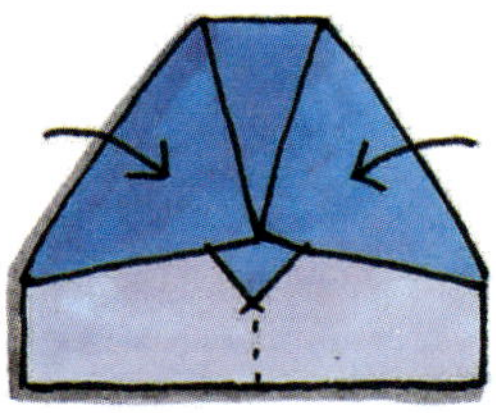

3 Fold in sides along dotted lines. Points must meet in centre.

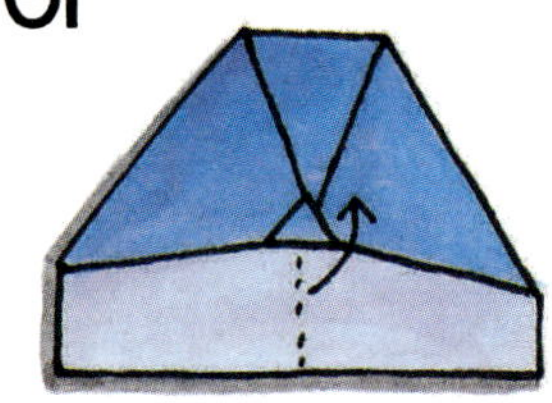

4 Fold up the small point.

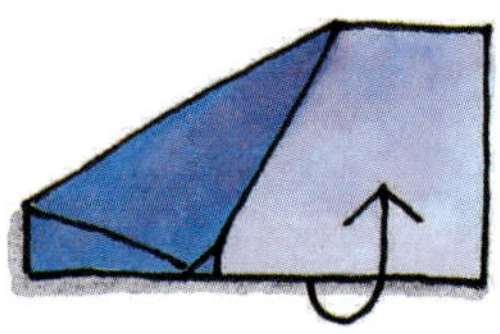

5 Fold in half outwards, along length.

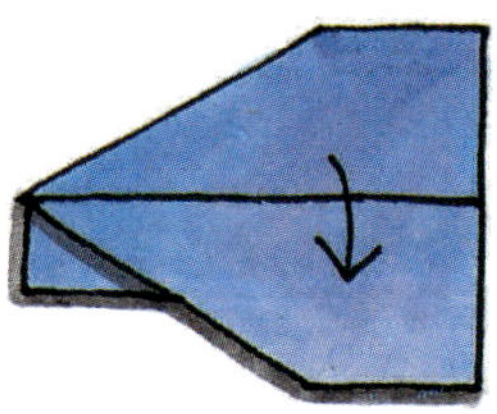

6 Fold wing down along dotted line.

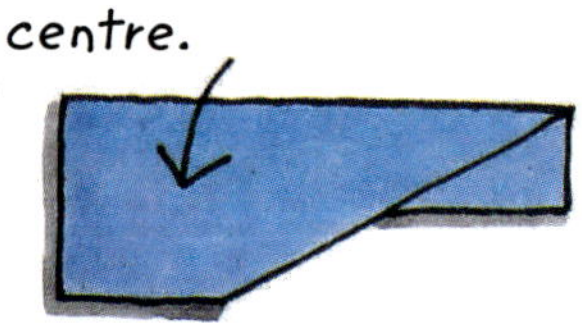

7 Turn over. Fold down other wing.

Square Wing

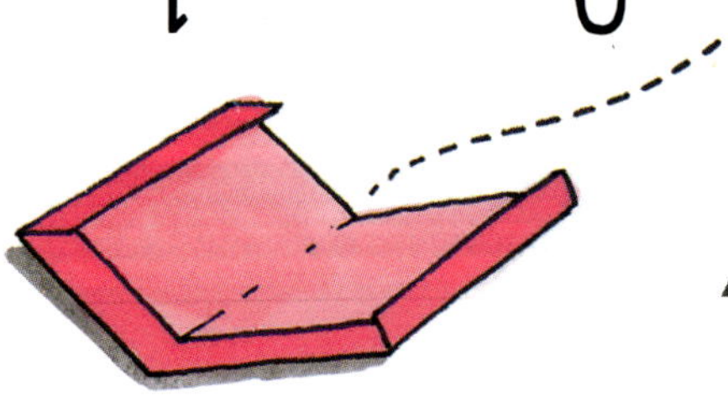

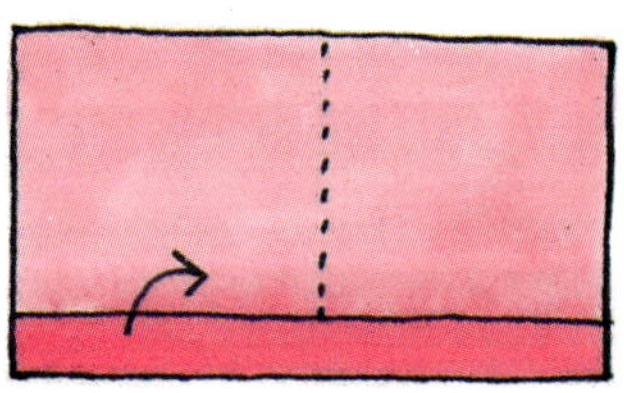

1 Fold long edge over, along dotted line. Repeat three times.

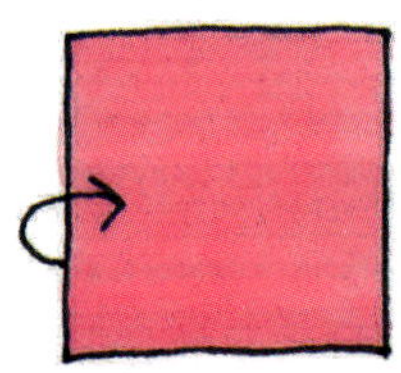

2 Fold in half, inwards.

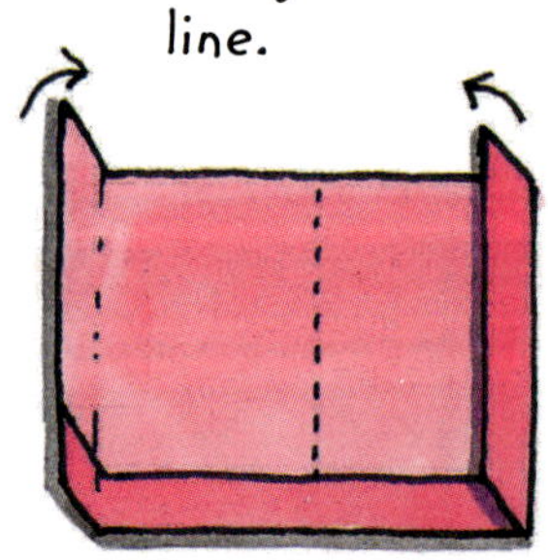

3 Open again. Fold each end in, along dotted line.

Decorating planes

Only use crayons, coloured pencils or felt tips to draw on your planes, as paint will make the paper wrinkly. Try not to crumple the planes while you are decorating them.

When making your own planes you can use coloured or patterned papers, too.

Camouflage

Draw wavy lines in pen or crayon. Colour in with greens and browns. You could make the underside sky-blue to camouflage it from below.

Stencils

Use the stencils to draw shapes on your planes, then colour them in. If you use the ring stencil, complete the circle after removing the stencil card.

Names

Give your plane a special name or a lucky number. Each time your plane wins a race you could draw a star or stroke on it, to keep track of how often it has won.

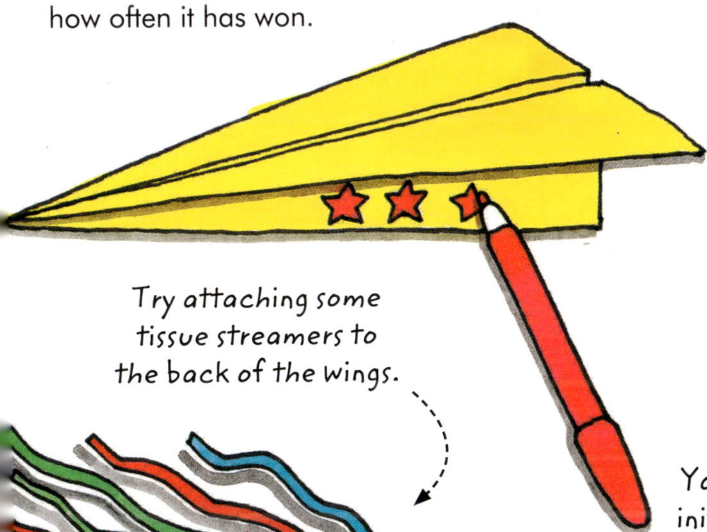

Symbols and logos

Airforces worldwide have special symbols, called insignia, which identify their planes. See if you can find out what they look like. You could design your own insignia to put on the planes you make. Here are some ideas:

You could use your initials in the design

Try attaching some tissue streamers to the back of the wings.

Add sticky shapes, but not too many or the plane will become too heavy to fly!

Creative planes

Plane mobiles

Use the templates to trace planes on to stiff paper (see page 2 for tips on tracing). Cut them out and decorate them. Make sure the underneath is interesting too. Attach thread to the top of the plane with sticky tape and hang from the ceiling (with adult help and permission!).

You could hang several planes and vary the lengths of the thread.

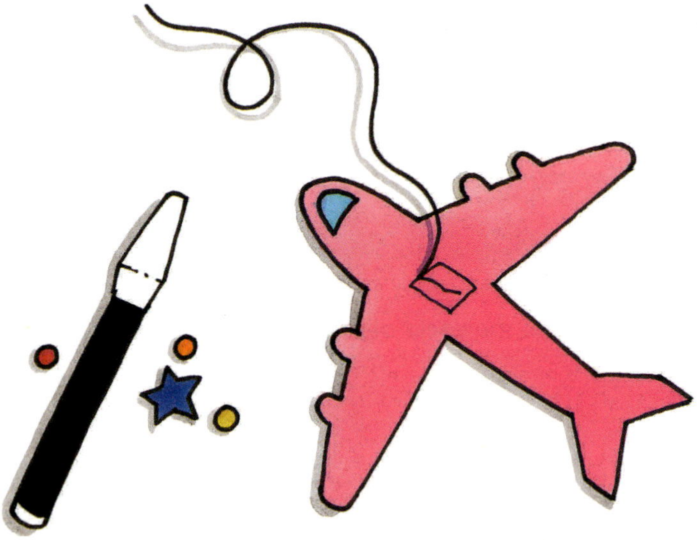

Cards and invitations

Using a template or stencil, press a plane outline on to silver paper with a biro. Cut it out and stick it on to coloured card. You could decorate the background with clouds.

How about inviting your friends to a plane race? Write the details in cloud shapes on the back of the card. All you will need is some A4 paper and a space for the race (see opposite).

Luggage labels

Use thick coloured paper, stickers and a pen to write your name, telephone number and holiday destination on the back. Even if you're not actually flying away on holiday, these plane labels will look great on your bag or rucksack.

Make a hole in the nose and thread string through it to tie your label.